For breakfast:

NOTE on BREAKFAST CEREALS:
it's much tastier and healthier to make
your own mix by buying several kinds of
flakes and cereal grains separately and
adding dried fruits and nuts, seeds, exotic
dried fruit, wheatgerm, powdered milk for
texture...

Ready made:

PASTRIES:
choose the ones that have real butter
and the least possible additives.

PESTOS:
are good and can be used
on pasta, put on fish to be
cooked in foil packets in
the oven, in cold rice for
a salad...

In the fridge:

GREEK-STYLE YOGURT
can be used in place
of cream in savory
or sweet dishes.
Very useful.

DIJON
MUSTARD

CREAM

BUTTER
salted or
unsalted

FRESH HERBS
parsley, chives, mint, coriander, etc, are a cheap
way to give a lift to the most ordinary of dishes.
*Rinse them and keep them wrapped in paper towels in
the bottom of the fridge.*

(fresh is
always best...)

YOUR FAVORITE SAUCE
Tabasco,
worcestershire,

& fresh fruit & vegetables *in season...*

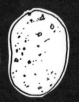

AVOCADOS

POTATOES

ORANGES

BERRIES (summer)

The Student's COOKBOOK

An illustrated guide to the essentials

Keda Black

Photography by Deirdre Rooney   Illustrations by Alice Chadwick

LYONS PRESS
Guilford, Connecticut
An imprint of Globe Pequot Press

Contents

Foreword

With little time, little money, and limited kitchen equipment, the gourmet life of a student is too often a boring story of toast and unhealthy takeout. There are so many other things to plan and think about when you are at school...

With this book, you need worry no more. If you keep a limited but wise selection of food in the cupboard and fridge, and stop by the market from time to time, you'll have just about everything you need to make up some interesting, filling, and healthy meals in no time.

What's that you say? « *But I can't even boil an egg!* » Just you wait and see: we'll show you how to make up something as basic as a sandwich, or how to cook an omelette. And for those who already have a few skills, this book has plenty of ideas to vary meals — whether using the stovetop, a toaster oven or, of course, a microwave. And some recipes require no cooking at all! Whether you're craving a *sweet* treat, WARM COMFORT FOOD, or a *filling breakfast* to start a big day, we have something for you, **meat-eaters**, *vegoes*, **FOOD JUNKIES**...

Every recipe has a photo to tempt you **and** illustrated « step-by-step » instructions to guide you through. You're going to love it!

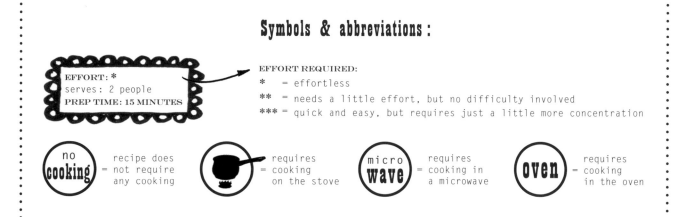

Symbols & abbreviations :

EFFORT: *
serves : 2 people
PREP TIME: 15 MINUTES

EFFORT REQUIRED:
* = effortless
** = needs a little effort, but no difficulty involved
*** = quick and easy, but requires just a little more concentration

no **cooking** recipe does = not require any cooking

requires = cooking on the stove

micro **wave** requires = cooking in a microwave

oven requires = cooking in the oven

Mozzarella, Tomato and More

 EFFORT: *
serves: 2 people
PREP TIME: 15 MINUTES

 no cooking

INGREDIENTS:

 2 small ripe tomatoes
+
 1 lemon
+
 1 ripe avocado*

 * 3-4 ripe fresh figs + 1 teaspoon clear honey **OR**

 OLIVE OIL

salt

& black pepper

2 balls of mozzarella*

good crusty bread

a few sprigs of fresh basil

*(buffalo mozzarella is a bit more expensive, but far more tasty)

EQUIPMENT:

 knife

chopping board

 Rinse the basil, cut off the leaves.

DRAIN mozzarella & cut into slices.

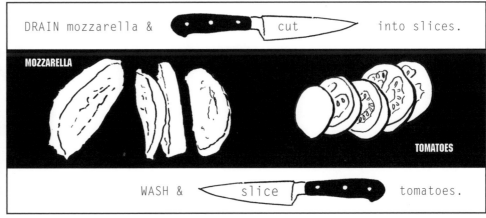 MOZZARELLA   TOMATOES

WASH & slice tomatoes.

 PEEL the avocado,

 SQUEEZE a few drops of lemon over it

 & CUT into slices.

 OR RINSE & SLICE the figs.

 On a plate, ARRANGE overlapping slices of tomato, avocado and mozzarella.

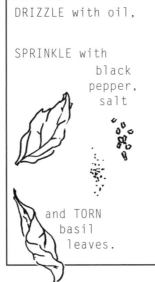 DRIZZLE with oil,

SPRINKLE with black pepper, salt

and TORN basil leaves.

ARRANGE overlapping slices of fig, tomato & cheese. DRIZZLE with oil & honey, SPRINKLE with salt, pepper & basil leaves.

You can leave the salad to MARINATE for about 30 minutes

 MARINATE 30 MIN

before serving with good crusty bread.

Real Tabouleh

INGREDIENTS :

Tbsp = tablespoon

1 handful **BULGUR WHEAT**
(about 1½ oz / ¼ cup)

2 spring onions or 1 shallot

1 bunch of flat-leaf parsley

1 bunch of mint

1-2 Tbsp OLIVE OIL

salt & pepper

1 lemon

EQUIPMENT:

chopping knife board

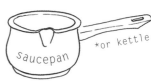

saucepan *or kettle

Optional :

 a ripe tomato

 a small chunk of cucumber

 a small piece of red pepper

 if in season, half a peach or 1 plum (ripe).

PLACE bulgur wheat in a bowl and cover with boiling water (about 6 fl oz / ¾ cup, or a **LARGE** glass).

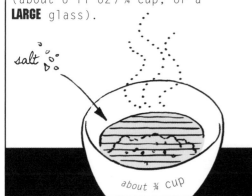

salt

about ¾ cup

Cover with

a plate

&

LEAVE ASIDE.

RINSE the herbs, PAT DRY between sheets of paper towels. DETACH leaves from stems. CHOP leaves finely. Discard stems.

CHOP finely.

PEEL & CHOP the onions finely. If using, CHOP the cucmber, tomato and / or red pepper into very small dice...

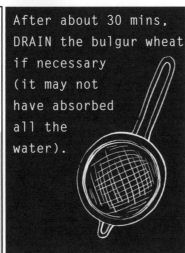

...as well as the peach or plum, if using.

After about 30 mins, DRAIN the bulgur wheat if necessary (it may not have absorbed all the water).

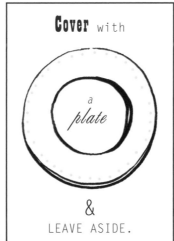

PUT it into a bowl. ADD:

the herbs   lemon juice

& the vegetables   oil

&   some pepper.

MIX *gently* with a fork.

TASTE & ADJUST the seasonings if necessary (*oil, lemon, pepper & salt*).

This tabouleh will be very green and not too filling. Eat as a salad or try with foil-baked fish for instance. It's ideal for a picnic or a packed lunch, along with some fresh cheese and a chunk of bread.

salad days

02

Super Salad — Chicken, Chickpeas & Bulgur Wheat

EFFORT: **
serves: 2 people
PREP TIME: 30 MINUTES

INGREDIENTS:

Tbsp = tablespoon
tsp = teaspoon

 1 small can of CHICK PEAS

 1 handful BULGUR WHEAT (about 2 oz / ¼ cup)

 1 chicken breast

 a good pinch of CUMIN seeds

 1 lemon

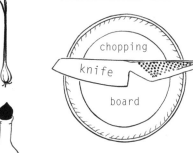 6 sprigs of fresh coriander

 1 spring onion (or 1 small shallot)

 pepper   salt

 OLIVE OIL 4 Tbsp (¼ cup)

EQUIPMENT:

 chopping knife board

 frying pan

 saucepan   *or kettle

---

PLACE bulgur wheat into a bowl

 with a little salt — water

POUR in about 6 fl oz / ¾ cup boiling water.

COVER with a plate...

&

LEAVE ASIDE.

DRAIN the chickpeas.

*it should be cooked through, check by cutting in half.

HEAT UP 1 Tbsp olive oil.
cumin   oil   chicken
ADD the chicken & cumin.

SEAR both sides

ADD a glass of water.

LOWER the heat *slightly* & SIMMER for about 15 minutes.

Cooking time depends on the thickness of the meat*.

Put onto a PLATE & CUT into small pieces.

MAKE a vinaigrette DRESSING in a screw-top jar:

3 Tbsp olive oil

shake

salt   pepper

2–3 tsp lemon juice

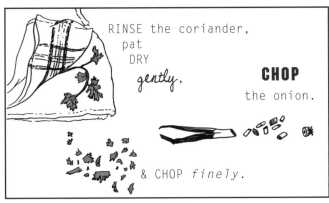

RINSE the coriander, pat DRY *gently*,

CHOP the onion.

& CHOP *finely*.

In a large bowl, COMBINE drained wheat, chickpeas, chopped onion, chicken pieces (along with cumin seeds) & vinaigrette.

sprinkle the coriander

MIX very gently.

>>> This salad is quite filling and makes for a light meal by itself!

salad days

03

Interesting Grated Carrots

INGREDIENTS :

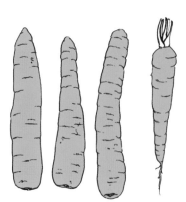

4 carrots
(preferably organic)

1
lemon

salt & pepper

OLIVE OIL
1-2 tablespoons
(about ⅛ cup)

EQUIPMENT :

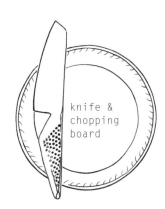
simple grater

knife & chopping board

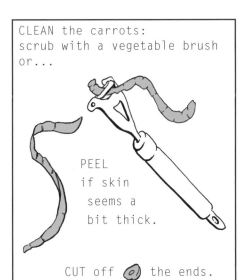

CLEAN the carrots:
scrub with a vegetable brush or...

PEEL if skin seems a bit thick.

CUT off ⬤ the ends.

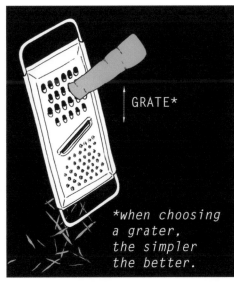

GRATE*

*when choosing a grater, the simpler the better.

ADD:

a few drops of *lemon juice*

salt + pepper

some olive oil

then...

...ADD one, or a combination, of the following ingredients:

a little orange juice (freshly squeezed)

a few sprigs of fresh herbs
(mint, coriander) chopped

a teaspoon of dijon mustard

a pinch of cinnamon

1 tablespoon of mixed or single toasted seeds or nuts (sesame, sunflower, pumpkin seeds, pine nuts, hazelnuts, shaved or grated coconut)

1 grated apple

1 grated turnip

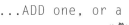

To TOAST seeds or nuts: heat a frying pan (without any oil) on a MEDIUM heat. When it is hot, throw in seeds or nuts and toast by shaking the pan gently. Remove from the pan, to a plate, as soon as they start to brown lightly.

shake (gently)

🐰 **Grated carrots** *are a year-round staple. Cheap and easy (you only need to own a grater, no need for anything electric or complicated), you won't ever get bored of this healthy starter if you set your imagination free, or simply go along with the few ideas above.*

Toasties

EFFORT: **
serves: 2 people
PREP TIME: 15 MINUTES

 oven *or* micro **wave**
with grill option   with grill option

INGREDIENTS:

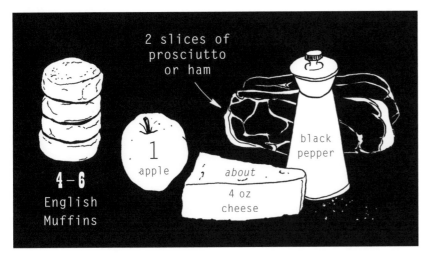

2 slices of prosciutto or ham

1 apple

black pepper

about 4 oz cheese

4 – 6 English Muffins

knife

EQUIPMENT:

CUT the apple into quarters and PEEL.

¼

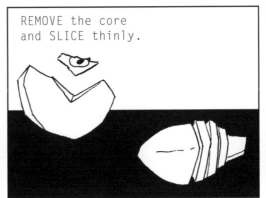

REMOVE the core and SLICE thinly.

SLICE the cheese.

----- GRILL -----

TOAST the muffins *very lightly*
(under a pre-heated grill or in the oven).

TOP the muffins with:

the slices of apple

the cheese

the ham*

*(fold it if necessary)

Add some black pepper and TOAST until the cheese melts and turns golden.

English Muffins are usually eaten with a lot of butter, and jam or honey. But they work very well with savory food too, the holes and unusual texture making a nice change from the everyday grilled cheese.

Try other combinations:

*cheese, ham, tomato

*blue cheese & apple, cooked ham

*or add the thinnest bit of crystallized (candied) ginger in the cheese and apple recipe

*if you like beets: cooked beets, thinly sliced: melted butter and cheddar: black pepper etc....

quick fix

How to cook an Omelette

EFFORT: ***
serves : 2 people
PREP TIME: 10 MINUTES

INGREDIENTS :

tsp = teaspoon

6 eggs

²/₃ oz /
4 tsp
butter

pepper
&
salt

EQUIPMENT:

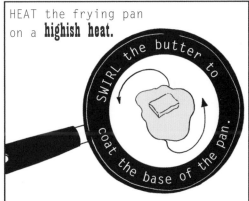

spatula

*or wooden spoon
or large wooden fork
(or silicone)*

frying
pan
*small or
medium**

**If the pan is too big, the egg
mixture will spread out too thinly
and the omelette will be dry. If
it is too small, the omelette will
be a bit too thick, but this is
a lesser evil as you will simply
have to cook the omelette a little
longer on a lower heat, at the risk
of making it a bit too dry on the
outside. A good omelette must remain
quite moist.*

BREAK the eggs...

into
a bowl.

---

*salt &
pepper*

MIX ever so slightly*

**do not beat, just
break the yolks. You're
not looking for a smooth
uniform mixture.*

HEAT the frying pan
on a **highish heat.**

SWIRL the butter to
coat the base of the pan.

When it starts to melt and
sizzle, TILT the pan so that the
melting butter covers the bottom
surface of the pan.

POUR in the eggs. WATCH THEM: as soon
as the edges look cooked...

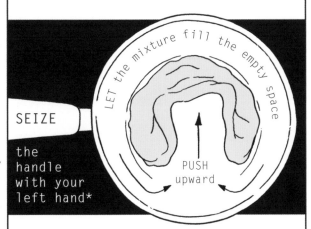

LET the mixture fill the empty space

SEIZE
the
handle
with your
left hand*

PUSH
upward

*(unless you are left-handed!)

TILT the pan slighly down toward you,
and with your right hand use a spatula
to PUSH the egg mixture up away from you.
Some of the uncooked mixture will crawl
down to the empty space you've made.
Tilt the pan back in place on the heat.

So, this is the time to ADD
any ingredients you have ready
to CUSTOMIZE your omelette:

chopped fresh herbs
(mint is surprising but good),

any type of **soft cheese**
(low fat cream cheese,
cottage cheese, ricotta,
goat cheese...), good with the
herbs too.

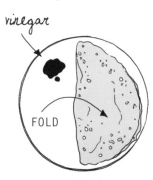

any type of
grated cheese.

VINEGAR

And of course, at
the end, on the plate,
a dash of **vinegar.**

TURN the heat off.
Use the spatula to
FOLD the omelette
in two and SLIDE it
onto a plate.

vinegar

FOLD

If *you only have a
very small frying
pan and are cooking
for two, make two
omelettes in a row,
one after the other.*

quick fix

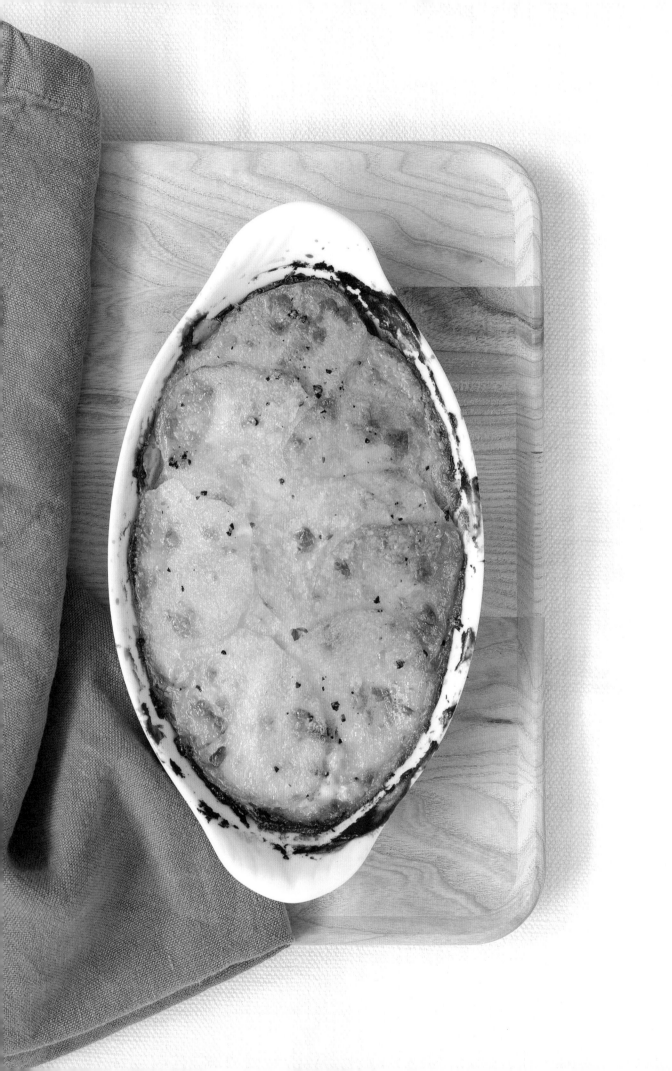

Potato Gratin

in the microwave

EFFORT: **
serves: 2 people#
PREP TIME: 40 MINUTES

#with leftovers for the next day

micro **wave** or oven

INGREDIENTS:

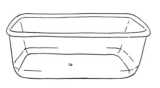
 about ... 1 lb potatoes

 1 clove of garlic

 salt
+
pepper

2 Tbsp butter

heavy cream **or** a mix of cream & milk

(10 fl oz/1¼ cups)

EQUIPMENT:

rectangular plastic box*
(microwavable)

or

rectangular or oval gratin dish*
(ovenproof)

*about 12 inches long

and

knife

 CUT

the garlic clove in **2** and...

...RUB the cut side all over the inside of the dish, followed by the butter.

garlic *butter*

PEEL and SLICE the potatoes as thinly as possible *(that's the longest part of the recipe).*

S-L-I-C-E

LAYER the potatoes in the dish, adding a little salt and pepper between layers.

salt
garlic
pepper

POUR over the cream* *(or the milk & cream)

If you like a slightly stronger garlicky taste, you can even add little bits of garlic between the layers.

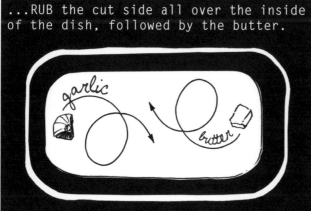

COOK in the microwave for about **20 minutes** — but this really depends on your own particular oven, the first time, keep an eye on it...

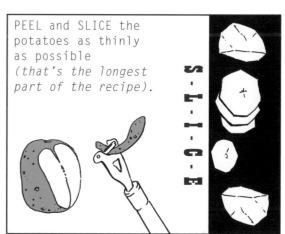

the potatoes should have absorbed all the liquid and be nice and creamy.

If it has a grill function, finish the gratin under the grill for 5-10 minutes.

This makes a satisfying gratin, quite moist and creamy. But you can make a lovely gratin the traditional way, using the same method but cooking it in an oven for about 1½ hours at a low temperature (320°F).

This is the *classic version* of a gratin dauphinoise.

You can add bits of cooked bacon

 or grated cheese.

quick fix

Baked Potatoes
healthy & quick

EFFORT: *
serves: 2 people
PREP TIME: 15 MINUTES

micro **wave** *or oven*

INGREDIENTS:

2 LARGE

potatoes

pepper
& salt

DRIED CHIVES

Sour CREAM

cheddar*
*grated

toppings

butter

EQUIPMENT:

grater

OR FOR THE OVEN:

metal knives *or skewers*

FOR THE MICROWAVE:

plastic box*

with a lid

*big enough for the potatoes

OR

ALUMINIUM FOIL

MICROWAVE:

WASH the potatoes *thoroughly* BUT do not dry!

PIERCE holes all over *with a knife*
pointed

PLACE in the microwave and COOK for
about 7-8 minutes.

*Potatoes should be tender when pierced with a knife but not completely soft.**

*You might need to adjust the cooking time according to the size of the potatoes and to your oven.

5 min

WRAP the potatoes in foil or place in a plastic container with a lid and LEAVE for 5 minutes outside the oven: this will finish the cooking.

OR

5 min

OVEN: *They will take at least an hour* at 400°F, *depending on the size of the potatoes.*

Pierce them with a metal skewer or knife, which you should leave in for cooking (*it will conduct the heat inside and speed up the process a little*).

attention!

DO NOT USE PLASTIC or WOOD!

Then once the potatoes are ready:

SLIT the skin & add the TOPPINGS...

Salted butter & black pepper is great.

Grated cheese is delicious.

pickle
OR TRY sour cream + chives or shredded cheese.

quick fix

Midnight Spaghetti

EFFORT: **
serves: 2 people
PREP TIME: 20 MINUTES

INGREDIENTS:

Tbsp = tablespoon

3 cloves of garlic

a good pinch
of dried chilies
(optional)

black
pepper

& salt

SPAGHETTI
1 oz

4 Tbsp
(¼ cup)

*olive
oil*

***

EQUIPMENT:

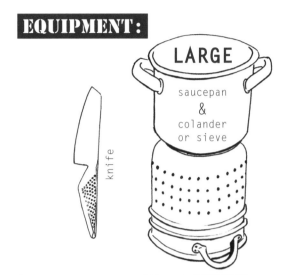

LARGE

saucepan
&
colander
or sieve

knife

TAKE OUT a **LARGE** pan and HEAT some water (<u>at least</u> 2 litres/70 fl oz/ 8 cups). When it reaches a rolling boil, ADD some...

SALT

8
cups
of water

...then
PLUNGE in
the pasta.

When the water comes back to a boil, check the time or put a timer on.*

*Follow guidelines from the packaging.

---

*While the
pasta is
cooking,*

PEEL
the
garlic
and
SLICE
as
thinly
as
possible.

the
cooked
pasta

a little
liquid

When your pasta is ready*, DRAIN it, but try to keep a little of the cooking liquid aside in a bowl.

*taste it: it should still be firm (al dente) — or not, cook it to your liking!

PUT the pan back on a medium heat and pour in the oil.

oil

garlic

chillies

→ ADD
the garlic and
chilies and
cook briefly
until garlic
just starts to
turn golden.

REMOVE from heat, ADD the drained pasta and reserved liquid.

MIX
with the
« sauce ».

MIX gently

A good recipe for when the fridge is empty. An all-time classic often called « **aglio olio** » *(garlic & oil).*

09

pasta night

Creamy Lemon Butter Pasta

EFFORT: **
serves: 2 people
PREP TIME: 15 MINUTES#

less if you use fresh pasta

INGREDIENTS :

of butter

4 Tbsp

(2 oz/ ½ stick)

PASTA (7 oz)

cream*

6 fl oz / ¾ cup

*(light or heavy)

salt

pepper

1 lemon*

*preferrably unwaxed or organic

EQUIPMENT:

grater or zester

lemon juicer

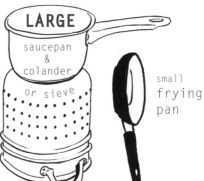

LARGE

saucepan & colander

or sieve

small frying pan

☞ This recipe also works with fresh pasta, which needs only a few minutes cooking.

BOIL water for the pasta: you need at least 4 cups per 3½ oz pasta. When it comes to a rolling boil, ADD the pasta and COOK for the required time.

pasta

salt

Rolling boil

← medium heat

While the pasta is cooking, WASH the lemon and GRATE its zest* finely   (use the fine side of a grater).

SQUEEZE the juice.

*The lemon zest gives an interesting taste but leave it out if you don't have a grater or if the skin of the lemon is too smooth to be grated.

DRAIN the cooked pasta.

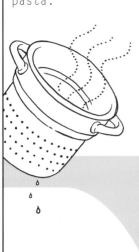

HEAT the butter in the pan   on a low heat. ADD:

half the lemon juice

the cream

the zest

2 min

ATTENTION!

LOW HEAT

LET this sauce SIMMER for about **2 MINUTES**. Taste and ADD more lemon if necessary, some SALT & PEPPER.

PUT the pasta in with the sauce & MIX

gently.

Serve & eat!

pasta night

10

Carbonara

EFFORT: **
serves: 2 people
PREP TIME: 20 MINUTES

INGREDIENTS:

4 slices of bacon
or pancetta

2 eggs

spaghetti, tagliatelle
or linguine

1 tablespoon
of butter

salt & pepper

2 oz of grated parmesan
or pecorino cheese

EQUIPMENT:

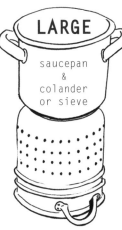

LARGE

saucepan
&
colander
or sieve

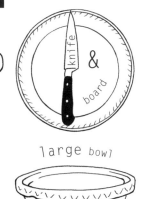

knife & board

large bowl

CUT the bacon or pancetta into cubes or strips.

HEAT the butter in the pan and FRY the bacon (or pancetta), STIRRING from time to time, until the pieces are lightly browned.*

MEDIUM HEAT

EMPTY onto a plate.

*Cook them longer if you like them crunchy.

PUT water to BOIL in the pan (at least 8 cups), with a little salt. When it reaches a **ROLLING** boil, ADD the pasta and COOK for the recommended time.

8 cups

Meanwhile, BREAK the eggs in a large bowl and MIX in the grated cheese.

Add the fried bacon.

DRAIN the pasta.

DRAIN a little earlier if you like your pasta firmer.

Tip pasta into a bowl and stir to COMBINE with the « egg-cheese-bacon » mixture. Add PEPPER.

Tips

1. There was no cream in the original recipe!

2. The egg mixture should never go on the stove. It will cook when it comes into contact with the hot pasta.

3. It's always best to buy cheese whole and grate it freshly at home. Buy parmesan shavings rather than the grated powder-like kind if you find it. But ready-grated will do!

Serve sprinkled with parmesan cheese.

Whole Wheat Pasta & Arugula

EFFORT: *
serves: 2 people
PREP TIME: 15 MINUTES

INGREDIENTS:

Tbsp = tablespoon
tsp = teaspoon

3½ oz

1 bag of **ARUGULA**

Tbsp

OLIVE OIL

(¼ cup)

TABASCO

or any form of chili

7 OZ OF WHOLE WHEAT SPAGHETTI

(or other pasta shapes)

salt

⅓ cup **(1½ oz)** of parmesan
(preferrably grated from a whole piece)

EQUIPMENT:

LARGE

saucepan
&
colander
or strainer

grater
or
peeler

COOK the pasta in a large quantity of salted boiling water (<u>at least</u> 8 cups) for the recommended time.

SALT

For 7 oz of pasta you need at least **8 cups** of water

...so it's better to use a **LARGE** saucepan.

GRATE the parmesan...

or

SHAVE with a peeler.

DRAIN the pasta (retaining a little of the cooking liquid).

cooked pasta

a little *liquid*

RETURN the pasta to tl

Add:

the chili

the liquid

the arugula

the oil

most of the parmesan

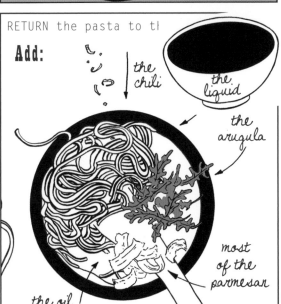

MIX gently...

&

serve sprinkled with the remaining parmesan.

Tips

1. You can make this with fresh baby spinach leaves (also available in a bag). The leaves will « cook » in the still hot pasta.

2. You can also vary the cheeses — use something fresh, like ricotta, for example.

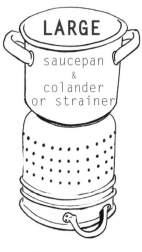

pasta night

12

SPRINKLE with peanuts
and torn mint
leaves

DIY Noodles

EFFORT: **
serves: 2 people
PREP TIME: 20 MINUTES

INGREDIENTS:

Tbsp = tablespoon
tsp = teaspoon

1 chicken breast

1 clove of garlic

and/or a piece of ginger

4 OZ of **Asian** *Noodles***
*not thin rice noodles

OIL 4 Tbsp
(¼ cup)

2 Tbsp SOY SAUCE
(⅛ cup)

2 Tbsp *VINEGAR*
(⅛ cup)

3 tsp of **SUGAR**

1 small carrot

eggs 2

1 small onion or 2 spring onions

a few sprigs of mint, rinsed

*rice, white wine, or cider vinegar... if you only have red wine vinegar, then use it!

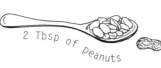
2 Tbsp of peanuts

EQUIPMENT:

large frying pan or wok

spoon or spatula
wooden or silicone

knife & chopping board

PRE-COOK the noodles according to the package instructions:

- some need soaking in cold water for 10 minutes
- others in boiling water
- some need actual cooking for a few minutes.

Then:
    DRAIN.

Meanwhile, CUT the chicken

into bite- sized pieces.

PEEL & CHOP *very finely*:

the onion
&
the carrot   the garlic.

PEEL

and GRATE
the ginger.

CHOP

the peanuts

or CRUSH them by putting them in a small plastic bag, TYING it with a knot, then CRUSHING them with a jar...

or rolling pin.

high HEAT

HEAT the oil in the pan or wok. FRY the chicken, on a high heat, stirring constantly with a wooden spoon, until it starts to brown. ADD: *the garlic, onion, carrot, soy sauce, vinegar, sugar and a small glass of water.* Keep STIRRING.

STIR

PUSH the ingredients to the side of the pan and BREAK the eggs into the empty space. STIR, breaking the yolks, then MIX in, little by little, the noodles and other ingredients.
COOK for 2-3 minutes STIRRING.

Transfer
to plates, SPRINKLE with the peanuts and torn mint leaves.

pasta night

Tips

1. You can leave out the chicken or substitute with any kind of protein: cubed tofu, shrimp, pieces of fish, turkey...

2. You can also add more vegetables, like fresh peas, chopped cabbage or bok choy, chopped broccoli... a good way to use any bits and pieces left in the fridge.

one pan Real Steak & Blue Sauce

INGREDIENTS:

Tbsp = tablespoon

1 large
or 2 smaller steaks

4 oz of
blue cheese

salt
& pepper

crème
fraîche
or
heavy cream

(5 FL OZ /
²/₃ CUP)

OIL

2 Tbsp

(⅛ cup)

EQUIPMENT:

frying
pan *or*
grill
pan

ALUMINIUM FOIL

spatula
or wooden spoon

OIL and lightly **pepper** the meat.

oil

HEAT the pan *gently*. LAY the meat in the hot pan. On a medium heat, COOK for about

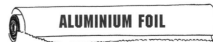

2 min* on each side.

*This depends on the thickness of the cut and how well you like your meat done.

ADD some **salt** and REMOVE to a plate. COVER with some foil (or an other plate) to keep warm.

WIPE the pan... with a paper towel.

PLACE back on a low heat. ADD cheese and cream and let everything MELT *slowly* and thicken a little.

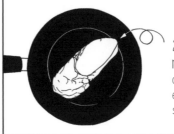

THE CREAM

low heat

POUR over the meat.

Eat with boiled potatoes, oven baked fries, a green salad. Or just a chunk of bread.

Plan B (if you don't like blue cheese) • ADD a little **water** to the pan once the meat has been removed (even a little **wine** if you have some open). ADD some **dijon mustard** and a little **salt**. Let this BOIL on a highish heat, SCRAPING the pan with the spatula, so that it reduces a little and makes a nice « jus » (juice, or sauce) for your meat.

in need of meat

mustardy & creamy Express Chicken

INGREDIENTS:

Tbsp = tablespoon

2 chicken breasts

1-2 Tbsp
(⅛ cup) of dijon mustard

4 Tbsp
(2 fl oz/ ¼ cup) of crème fraîche or sour cream

salt & pepper

frying pan

2 Tbsp (⅛ cup) oil

HEAT the oil in a frying pan, on a medium heat. PUT the chicken in the pan, laying it flat, and COOK on one side until *lightly golden*.

oil

TURN OVER

& cook the other side.

LOWER the heat. ADD the mustard and cream, MIXING everything *gently* together in the pan. LET the chicken finish cooking:

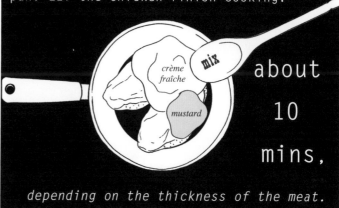

crème fraîche   mix

mustard

about 10 mins,

depending on the thickness of the meat.

To test if the chicken is cooked:

1: PIERCE with a knife: the juices should run clear,

<u>not</u> pink.

clear juice

2: If you are not sure, CUT right through the chicken: there should be no traces of *pink.*

Serve the chicken by POURING the sauce over it, SCRAPING the frying pan clean.

SEASON with salt & pepper and eat with bread, rice or potatoes, and maybe some salad too.

Turkey & Avocado

EFFORT: **
serves : 2 people
PREP TIME: 15 MINUTES

INGREDIENTS:

Tbsp = tablespoon

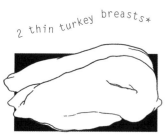

2 thin turkey breasts*

*Preferrably flattened down by the butcher.

1 avocado

1 lemon

or lime

TABASCO *(optional)*

3-4 Tbsp (¼ cup) of Greek-style yogurt

or cream or crème fraîche

salt & pepper

EQUIPMENT:

frying pan

& **1 Tbsp of oil**

PEEL and CUT the avocado into LARGE chunks.

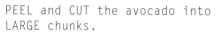

It's ok if large solid pieces remain, it doesn't need to be a purée, just a little smashed.

MASH roughly with a fork, *adding lemon juice to prevent it from blackening,* and ADD:

some TABASCO

salt & pepper

HEAT the oil in a pan, on a highish heat.

Brown the meat on one side, then the other.

turkey breasts

The turkey should cook in about **10 minutes,** *if the breasts are thin enough, otherwise lower the heat and leave to cook a little longer.*

When it is cooked, **LOWER the heat** and ADD the mashed avocado and yogurt, cream or crème fraîche.

Stir....

& REMOVE from the heat **quickly** (you don't want to actually cook the avocado).

Serve...

with potatoes

or rice, for example.

« Not Quite » Fish Fingers

EFFORT: **
serves: 2 people
PREP TIME: 30 MINUTES

 oven

INGREDIENTS:

Tbsp = tablespoon
tsp = teaspoon

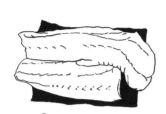

2 fish fillets
(any kind you like)

salt & pepper

4Tbsp
(½ stick) of butter

 1 lemon

6 Tbsp (½ cup) of breadcrumbs

EQUIPMENT:

 oven dish

grater or zester

saucepan

& to make this more interesting:

a few sprigs of fresh herbs of your choice, rinsed, dried, chopped

1 very finely chopped spring onion or shallot

 1 tsp of paprika or a pinch of cayenne pepper

zest of the lemon

a small piece of fresh ginger, peeled and grated

 a dash of Tabasco or chilli sauce

---

Place the fish fillets in an oven dish.

PREHEAT **the oven** to **425°F**

SPRINKLE with breadcrumbs. SEASON.

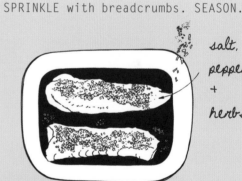

salt, pepper + herbs

ADD the ingredients of your choice: the chopped herbs, spices.

MELT the butter in a small saucepan. ADD:

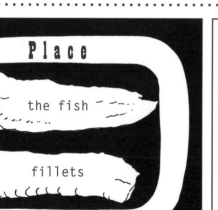

half the *juice of the lemon*

TABASCO

*the ginger**

*the zest**

*the onion**

*if you wish.

POUR ... over the fish.

COOK for **10-15** mins, depending on the thickness of the fish.

The cooked fish should flake easily with **a fork** but should still remain quite firm...

fish fix

17

Sardine Butter

EFFORT: *
serves: 2 people
PREP TIME: 10 MINUTES

no cooking

INGREDIENTS:

Tbsp = tablespoon

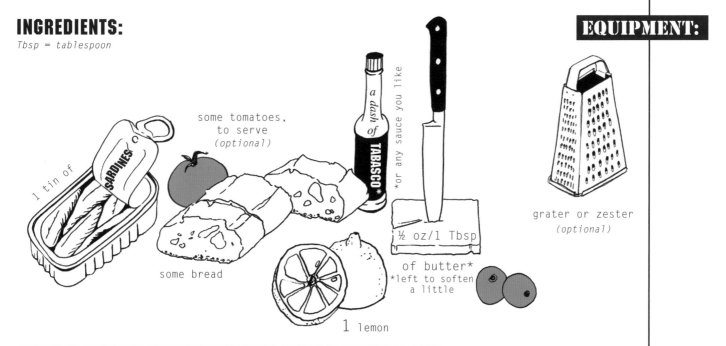

1 tin of SARDINES

some tomatoes, to serve *(optional)*

some bread

a dash of TABASCO *
*or any sauce you like

½ oz/1 Tbsp of butter*
*left to soften a little

1 lemon

EQUIPMENT:

grater or zester *(optional)*

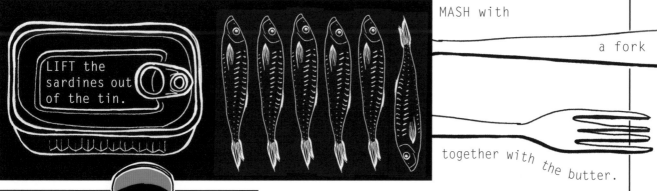

LIFT the sardines out of the tin.

MASH with a fork together with the butter.

ADD...

a dash of your favorite sauce

a little lemon juice

& the zest *(optional)*

MIX...

Serve with some bread and tomatoes.

A QUICK SNACK

fish fix

Smoked Mackerel Pâté

EFFORT: *
serves: 2 people
PREP TIME: 10 MINUTES

no cooking

INGREDIENTS:

1 smoked mackerel fillet

4 fl oz/ ½ cup

COTTAGE CHEESE

or fromage frais or thick yogurt

some chives* (optional)

fresh bread or toast

1 lemon

*or you could use cottage cheese with chives

EQUIPMENT:

knife & chopping board

grater or zester (optional)

CHOP the chives.

GRATE* the lemon zest.

*If you have one.

Using a fork, MASH the fish with the cheese or yogurt.

ADD...

a little lemon juice

the chives

the zest

MIX...

Eat spread on bread or toast.

I like to swim

Smoked mackerel is cheap and very tasty. Eat cold, in a salad, or hot with some boiled potatoes, or as a spread, as in this recipe. You can also use it as a dip for carrots or other vegetables.

fish fix

Raw Fish « Tahitian Style »

EFFORT: *
serves: 2 people
PREP TIME: 45 MINUTES#

includes 30 mins resting time

no cooking

INGREDIENTS :

1 very fresh
fish fillet
(7 oz)

5 fl oz/²⁄₃ cup
of coconut milk

salt & pepper

2-3 limes

¼ of a cucumber

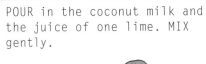

1 carrot

EQUIPMENT:

knife &
chopping board

grater

dish

DICE the fish.

REMOVE
any bones.

PLACE in a dish.
SEASON with:

some salt **&** pepper.

POUR in the coconut milk and
the juice of one lime. MIX
gently.

TASTE the marinade and
ADD more juice if necessary.
Leave to REST for about
<u>30 minutes.</u>

Meanwhile, PEEL and GRATE
the carrot and cucumber
with the coarse side
of the grater.

Mix gently

with the fish.

Eat with some bread

or...

rice.

Tip This is a very basic recipe for raw fish. The fish is actually « cooked » by the lime juice, so if you prefer the taste and texture of really raw fish, don't let it marinate for too long!
Plan B You can customize this recipe by adding some crushed garlic, a little finely grated fresh ginger, a dash of soy sauce, a dash of spicy sauce. OR sprinkle with some sesame or poppy seeds...

Green Fish Curry

the easiest possible

EFFORT: **
serves: 2 people
PREP TIME: 25 MINUTES

micro **wave**
or
optional

INGREDIENTS:

Tbsp = tablespoon; tsp = teaspoon

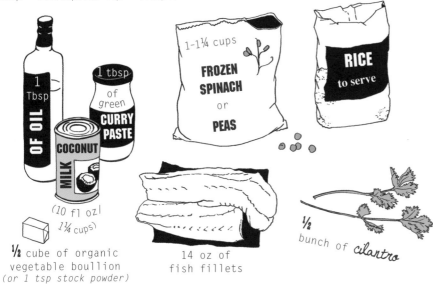

1 Tbsp OF OIL

1 tbsp of green CURRY PASTE

COCONUT MILK
(10 fl oz / 1¼ cups)

½ cube of organic vegetable boullion (or 1 tsp stock powder)

1–1¼ cups FROZEN SPINACH or PEAS

RICE to serve

14 oz of fish fillets

½ bunch of *cilantro*

EQUIPMENT:

SAUCEPAN

OR

microwavable container for the rice

large frying pan*

*or LARGE saucepan or wok

wooden spoon

COOK the rice...

on the stove

or in the microwave.

CUT the fish

into **LARGE**

cubes.

HEAT the oil in a large pan.

ADD the curry paste & FRY,

on a high heat, stirring with a wooden spoon,

for about 30 seconds.

30 SEC

l'huile

COCONUT MILK

ADD: the stock & a large glass of water.

BRING to a boil.

STIR to dissolve the stock, and LOWER the heat to a *gentle* simmer.

ADD the fish and the vegetables, COOK for about **5** to **10** minutes, depending on the size of the pieces of fish...

taste!

RINSE the cilantro, pat DRY with a paper towel and pick off the leaves. SPRINKLE onto the curry.

Serve with the rice.

You can use one type of fish or a combination.

Serve with croutons & ice cubes...

A very simple Gazpacho-style Soup

EFFORT: *
serves: 2 people
PREP TIME: 20 MINUTES

no cooking

INGREDIENTS:

Tbsp = tablespoon

  6 *ripe tom -a- toes*

  1 red pepper

1 onion

 1 CUCUMBER

   pepper

spicy sauce

6 ice cubes

&

12 croutons

OLIVE OIL 3 tbsp

+ salt

EQUIPMENT:

  SAUCEPAN*

*or kettle for boiling water

hand-held mixer or blender

BOIL some water. PUT the tomatoes in a large bowl or pan

&

COVER with the boiling water.

STAND for a few minutes.

PEEL off the skin.

CUT into **CHUNKS**.

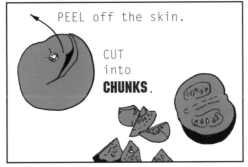

PEEL the cucumber & CUT into chunks.

REMOVE the white parts of the pepper... & the seeds.

Then CUT into chunks.

 PEEL the onion

& CUT into chunks.

Put all the vegetables in the mixer or blender and PROCESS. ADD some water if necessary &...

Chill in the fridge.
Serve with croutons and ice cubes.

the oil

some salt + pepper

some sauce

veggie forever

• This is the simplest possible recipe for a gazpacho-style summer soup. It is also nice to add bits of stale bread, or chopped herbs (some mint maybe) or even some summer fruit: chunks of melon, watermelon or ripe peach give an interesting twist.
• You could also save some whole bits of vegetable, cut them into tiny dice and lay them on top of the soup just before serving.

Red Lentil Soup
all-in-one

EFFORT: *
serves: 2 people
PREP TIME: 30 MINUTES#

#(including 20 mins cooking)

micro **wave**

INGREDIENTS:

tsp = teaspoon

7 OZ/ ¾ CUP OF **RED LENTILS***

(available in most supermarkets, health food or Indian shops)

a can of **TOMATOES**

1 onion

1 clove of garlic

2 tsp of spice *(garam masala or curry powder, or ras el hanout)*

COCONUT

CURRY 2 tsp

3 fl oz/½ cup coconut milk *(or Greek-style yogurt)*

1 lemon **or** lime

pepper

salt

EQUIPMENT:

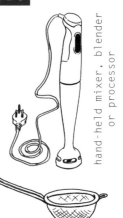

LARGE saucepan

or

large microwave

hand-held mixer, blender or processor

container

strainer

RINSE the lentils in a strainer.

PEEL and CUT the onion and garlic into large **CHUNKS**...

(or more finely if you don't have a blender or mixer).

PLACE all the ingredients in a large saucepan *(except the lime and coconut milk or yogurt).*

ADD 3 large glasses of water.

BRING to a *gentle boil*

Cook for about 20 minutes.   **The lentils will break down.**

---

blend the soup

if you don't have one, it will be fine as it is.

ADD:

a little lime or lemon juice

pepper

salt

most of the coconut milk* *or yogurt

*or yogurt

VERY LOW   **HEAT**

ADD...

the rest of the coconut milk or yogurt

SERVE.

You can make this soup in the microwave by putting all the ingredients (except the coconut milk and lemon) in a container and cooking on medium power for about 10 minutes (depending on your microwave).

veggie forever

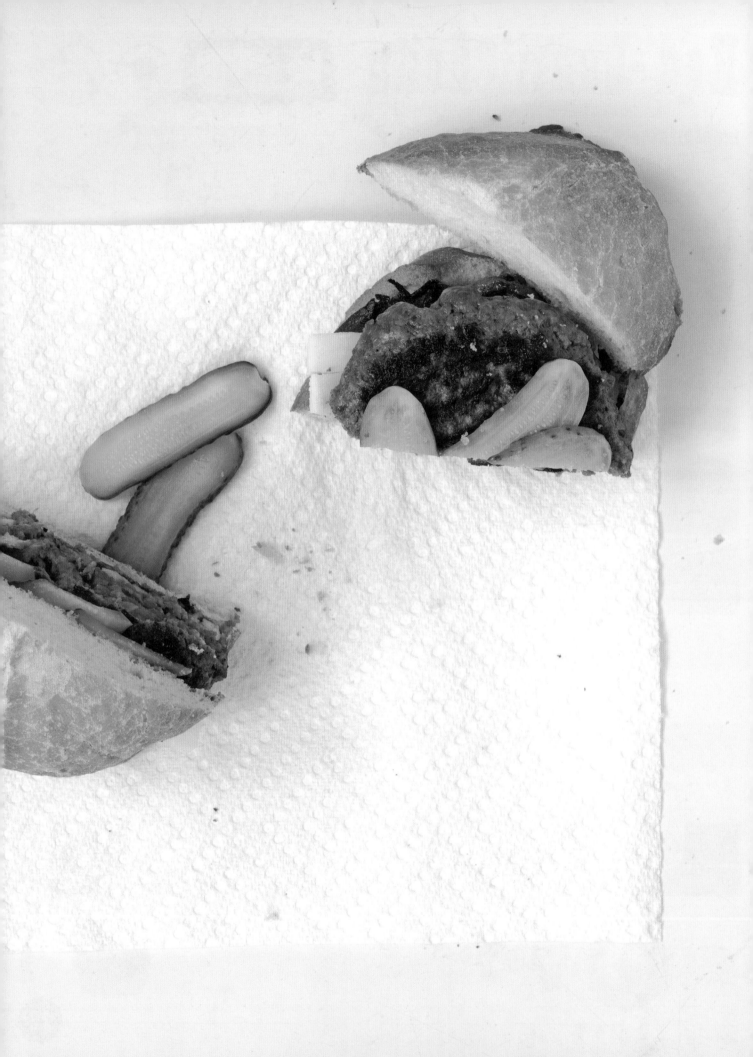

Homemade Burger

EFFORT: **
serves: 2 people
PREP TIME: 15 MINUTES

grill &
or toaster

INGREDIENTS:

Tbsp = tablespoon

2 burger buns

salt + pepper

1 tbsp OIL

SOME KETCHUP

SAUCE

a dash of worcestershire sauce *(or chili sauce, steak sauce, bbq sauce...)*

12-14 oz of GROUND BEEF

or 2 nice steaks or 2 pieces of beef fillet

2 slices of aged cheddar cheese

PICKLED GHERKINS

1 small onion or 1 Tbsp of onion jam

EQUIPMENT:

+ *a choice of:*

4-6 slices of cooked beets

OR 1 ripe avocado

OR 5 oz of blue cheese

frying pan

TOAST the buns.

PEEL and SLICE the onion

t h i n l y .

GROUND BEEF:

COMBINE the meat with the sauce and SEASON with salt and pepper...

MIX

SHAPE into burgers.

COOK in a frying pan,

on a medium to high heat, with a little oil.

STEAKS:

Or COOK the steaks in the oil...

...**then** SEASON with salt, pepper and the sauce.

MAKE UP the burgers:

half a bun

the extras: avocado

or beets

or blue cheese

more sauce?   *more cheese?*

the meat

the cheese slices

the onion slices *or onion jam*

a little ketchup   sliced pickled gherkins

half a bun

not so junk

Homestyle Club Sandwich

EFFORT: **
serves: 2 people
PREP TIME: 15 MINUTES

INGREDIENTS:

tsp = teaspoon

4 slices of bread

an avocado

2 tsp of vinegar

2 slices of bacon or cooked ham

EQUIPMENT:

frying pan

(optional)

knife

2 eggs

salad sprouts (alfalfa, watercress or similar, *optional*)

a little worcestershire sauce or Tabasco

some cream cheese with or without chives*

2-4 salad leaves

small SAUCEPAN

or some hummus, mayo, etc.

---

6 mins

PUT the eggs in a pan of water. BRING to a boil and cook for 6 mins *on a gentle boil.*

← cold water

PEEL

CUT in 2

PLACE under cold running water and SHELL. CUT the eggs in half.

---

vinegar

PEEL the avocado and CUT into slices, SPRINKLE with a little vinegar.

---

medium

HEAT

COOK the bacon, if using, in a small frying pan.

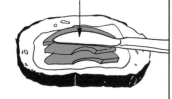

Press

SPREAD some cream cheese (or hummus, mayo, etc.) onto a slice of the bread. LAY the slices of avocado on top, then PRESS *lightly* with a knife.

SPRINKLE over a little sauce, then PUT the bacon or ham on. PLACE the eggs on top of the bacon or ham.

the *eggs*

the bacon

ADD the salad leaves and sprouts (they give some crunch and, depending on the variety, a little heat too).

Finish with a second slice of bread (with more spread, if you like)

&...

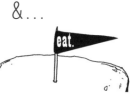

eat.

not so junk

25

Easy Hummus

EFFORT: **
serves: 6 people##
PREP TIME: 15 MINUTES

no **cooking** or optional

you can multiply the quantities if you have more guests

INGREDIENTS:

Tbsp = tablespoon
tsp = teaspoon

1 can of chick-peas

1 lemon

2-3 Tbsp (¼ cup) of olive oil

(optional) 1 Tbsp of PEANUT BUTTER

1 small clove of garlic

1 Tbsp of shredded coconut (optional)

pepper   salt

...and a few sprigs of cilantro or mint (optional)

EQUIPMENT:

lemon juicer

LARGE bowl

strainer

& knife board

potato masher or a fork

grater or zester

DRAIN the chickpeas...

I am RE-CYCLABLE!

reserving some of the liquid.

NOTE: MAKE sure to grate only the yellow skin, not the thick bitter white skin.

GRATE ½ tsp of lemon zest.

CUT the lemon in 2 and squeeze the juice.

PEEL the garlic and CRUSH the clove with the flat side of a knife.

CRUSH

CHOP very *finely*.

TRANSFER to a small bowl,

& SPRINKLE with the chopped herbs.

... or some toasted shredded coconut.*

*Throw coconut into an ungreased hot frying pan and stir for barely a minute until lightly browned. Take off the heat immediately as it burns very quickly.

stir!
medium heat

Serve with bread and raw vegetable sticks...

Or use as a spread on bagels or in a sandwich, with a little grated carrot and some leftover chicken.

MASH

ADD the peanut butter if you have it.

salt & pepper

MASH the chickpeas with 2 Tbsp of the oil, the lemon zest, the garlic & about

---

ADD a little of the canned chickpeas liquid if the mixture seems a bit dry.

THE texture of your mixture won't be as smooth as in usual hummus, but that's what makes it interesting!

Super Salsa **for Nachos**

no **cooking**

INGREDIENTS:

EQUIPMENT:

6 ripe tom -a- toes

half a bunch of cilantro (optional)

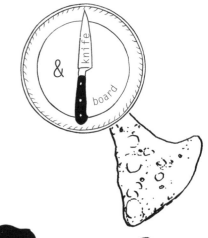

knife & board

 **1**
small onion
or 2 spring
onions

 1 small
*red chili**
*or some
Tabasco

 **1**
lime

 **PEPPER**
& salt

a shot of
tequila or vodka

 Alternatively: a small bunch of grapes OR ¼ of a ripe mango

DICE
the tomatoes
as small as
possible.

REMOVE the seeds from the chili

&

chop into *tiny pieces.*

PEEL

the onion and chop
very finely.

RINSE, DRY & CHOP

the cilantro.

CHOP the fruit, if using,
into small pieces.

MIX together all
of the ingredients,
using only a small amount   of *chili*

& a little *lime juice...*

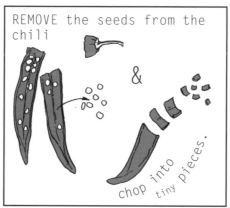

... THEN
add more if necessary.

Sexy Oatmeal

EFFORT: *
serves: 2 people
PREP TIME: 10 MINUTES

 *or* micro **wave**

INGREDIENTS:

Tbsp = tablespoon

medjool dates = a variety of dates, bigger, fatter, darker and better than the normal ones... if you can find them...or use "regular" dates...

14 fl oz/ 1⅔ cups *of* milk

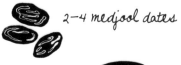 *2-4 medjool dates*

rolled oats

3-4 oz

or some jam **SOME HONEY** *  **OR** *some sugar*

a pinch of salt

2 tbs of cream*

OR

optional Greek-style Yogurt*

OR

2 Tbsp of butter

EQUIPMENT:

SAUCEPAN

OR

microwavable container

with a lid

knife

MICROWAVE :

PUT the oats in a microwavable container with a lid.

ADD the milk & ½ cup of water

the salt

the dates*

COOK on **medium power** for about

STIR

COOK AGAIN on **medium power** for a further

1½ to 2 min.

1 min. **OR**

STOVE :

PUT the oats in a saucepan.
ADD:

the milk & water*

½ cup

the salt

the dates*

BRING to a boil then reduce the heat, STIR and cook...

...until the oatmeal reaches a **thick** *consistency.*

STIR from time to time

on a *low* heat

Then... *whatever the method used,* ADD the honey, jam or sugar and the cream, yogurt or butter

& eat.

---

*To prepare the dates:

 cut them lengthwise, *& remove the pits.*

DELICIOUS WITH >>> some blueberries or raspberries, fresh or frozen, instead of dates. Or with some maple syrup instead of the honey!

3 Smoothies

Banana Strawberry Lassi

INGREDIENTS :

1 banana

2 natural yogurt

1 lemon or lime

1 basket (8 oz) of strawberries

EQUIPMENT:

blender

knife

RINSE & HULL the strawberries.

CUT them into pieces.

PEEL the banana & SLICE.

BLEND with the yogurt & a little lemon or lime juice.

Mango Dream

INGREDIENTS :

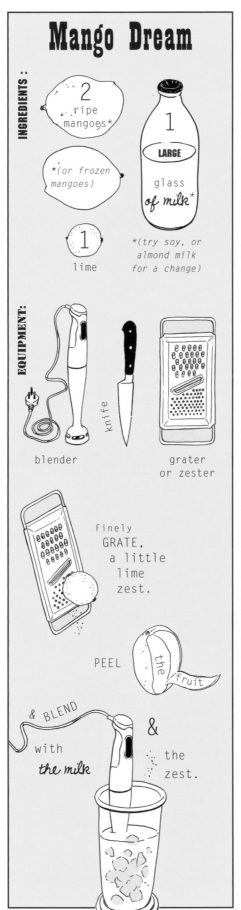

2 ripe mangoes*

*(or frozen mangoes)

1 lime

1 LARGE glass of milk*

*(try soy, or almond milk for a change)

EQUIPMENT:

blender

knife

grater or zester

Finely GRATE, a little lime zest.

PEEL the fruit

& BLEND with the milk & the zest.

Middle Eastern

INGREDIENTS :

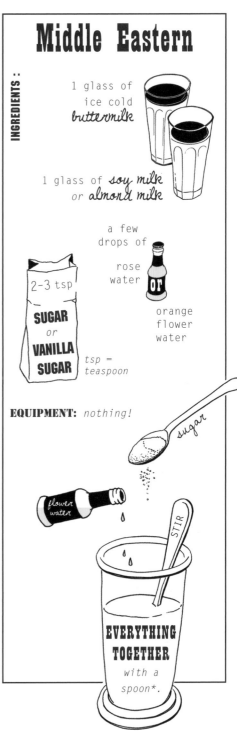

1 glass of ice cold buttermilk

1 glass of soy milk or almond milk

2-3 tsp SUGAR or VANILLA SUGAR

tsp = teaspoon

a few drops of rose water **or** orange flower water

EQUIPMENT: nothing!

sugar

flower water

STIR

EVERYTHING TOGETHER with a spoon*.

* You can mix it in a blender to get a more frothy texture, but it's fine to just mix everything together with a spoon!

Bread & Butter Pudding

EFFORT: **
serves: 2 people
PREP TIME: 50# or 25## MIN

micro **wave**
or oven

 # in the oven: 35 mins cooking time
in the microwave: 10 mins cooking time

INGREDIENTS:

Tbsp = tablespoon

6

slices
of stale bread

1¾ oz/
⅓ stick
of butter

some JAM
or marmalade (optional)

4-5 Tbsp
(¼ cup)
of **SUGAR**

12 fl oz/
1½ cups
of milk
or a mix
of milk
and cream

EQUIPMENT:

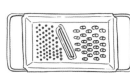

oven dish

or

microwavable
container

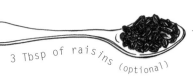

3 Tbsp of raisins (optional)

+

a little
RUM
or orange
juice

3 eggs

1 lemon

(optional)

grater or zester

PREHEAT the oven to 350°F.

PUT the raisins in the juice   or rum.

BUTTER the dish or microwave container.

butter

BUTTER the bread

& SPREAD
with the jam.

CUT each slice in half,

CUT diagonally

ARRANGE the slices in the dish or container, so that they point up a little.

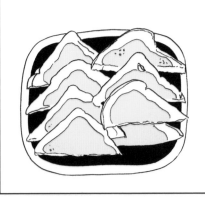

BEAT together*

the milk
(and/or cream)
+
the eggs
+
2-3 Tbsp
of sugar.

*with a whisk or fork.

GRATE the lemon zest. ADD the zest and the soaked raisins. POUR over the bread*.

SPRINKLE the top with the remaining sugar.

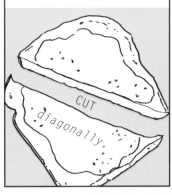

COOK **in the oven** for about 35 minutes. *It should be set and golden on top.*
COOK **in the microwave** on medium power for about **5 minutes**, then LET STAND inside the microwave for another **5 minutes**. *The pudding should be set, but will not brown like in a conventional oven.*

*the tips of the bread should ideally stick out.

sweet tooth

30

What a Mess!

EFFORT: *
serves: 2 people
PREP TIME: 10 MINUTES

no cooking

INGREDIENTS:

Tbsp = tablespoon
tsp = teaspoon

1 LARGE meringue*
*shop bought

1 tub of *low-fat cream cheese* 8 OZ

6 tbs of *crème fraîche or mascarpone*

1 basket (8 oz) of fresh berries:
raspberries, blueberries, blackberries,
strawberries, red currants etc, or a combination

EQUIPMENT:

2 glasses

LARGE bowl

fork

BREAK *the meringue* into **LARGE** pieces.

PREPARE the fruit:

RINSE* *if necessary

HULL & REMOVE any stems.

remove

PUT all the ingredients into a bowl

& STIR, *very gently**

you don't need to blend it, you merely want to combine the ingredients and crush the berries lightly so that their juice starts to mix with everything else.

TRANSFER into **2** glasses.

PUT into the fridge for a while or **eat** *immediately.*

Instant Chocolate Mousse

EFFORT: *   serves: 2 people   PREP TIME: 5 MINUTES

COMBINE **2** containers of Greek-style yogurt with

1 Tbsp of **cocoa powder**
(if unsweetened, add 2 tsp of sugar)

& STIR *vigorously...*

sweet tooth

31

Pretend Trifle

EFFORT: **
serves: 2 people
PREP TIME: 20 MINUTES

no cooking

INGREDIENTS:

Tbsp = tablespoon

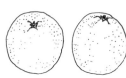

2 oranges

some cognac, sweet wine or a dash of Grand Marnier...

2 thick slices of shop-bought pound or butter cake

2 Tbsp of SUGAR*

or more if you like it sweet

EQUIPMENT:

2 bowls

whisk

⅔ cup 5 fl oz of light cream

& 4 oz of Greek-style yogurt

1 basket of strawberries (8 oz)

1 banana

large bowl for mixing

PUT a piece of cake into each of the two bowls.

alcohol + juice

x2

POUR over... ...the alcohol and the juice from the oranges.

RINSE and HULL the strawberries,

keeping aside 2 nice ones to decorate.

1
2

CUT the rest into pieces,

& PUT on top of the cake.

PEEL and SLICE the banana, and ADD to the strawberries.

In another bowl, WHIP the cream until it forms soft peaks*.

ADD the sugar & the yogurt.

Put into the bowls. DECORATE with the saved strawberries.

sweet tooth

Light cream whips up better when it is very cold. If necessary, put it in the freezer for a short while beforehand (but don't forget it!).

Citus Salad

EFFORT: *
serves: 2 people
PREP TIME: 15 MINUTES

no cooking

INGREDIENTS:

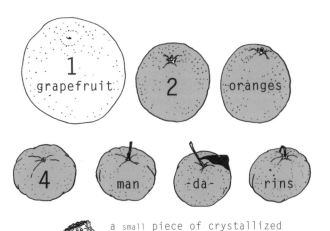

1 grapefruit

2 oranges

4 man- -da- -rins

a small piece of crystallized (candied) ginger *(optional)*

EQUIPMENT:

knife & board

large bowl

PEEL the grapefruit:

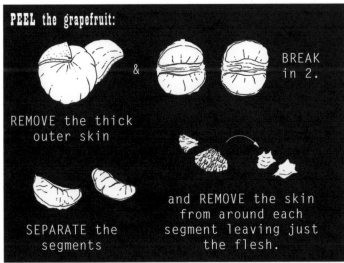

& BREAK in 2.

REMOVE the thick outer skin

SEPARATE the segments

and REMOVE the skin from around each segment leaving just the flesh.

PEEL the oranges with a knife...

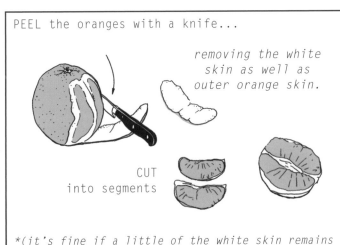

removing the white skin as well as outer orange skin.

CUT into segments

(it's fine if a little of the white skin remains as it is less bitter than the grapefruit skin).

PEEL the mandarins

& CUT with a knife

into 4 or 6 pieces.

PUT all of the fruit into a bowl.

CUT the ginger into tiny pieces and...

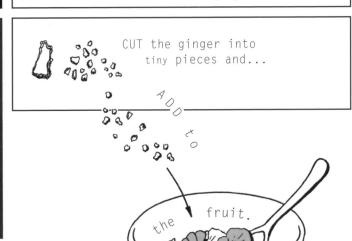

ADD to the fruit.

The sugar crystals from the ginger will dissolve in the juice and release a very subtle ginger flavor.

nice 'n' fruity

33

Wake-Up Strawberries
" 4 Ways "

EFFORT: **
serves: 2 people
PREP TIME: 15 MINUTES #

+ ideally 30 mins rest time

  no cooking *or*

INGREDIENTS:

Tbsp = tablespoon; tsp = teaspoon

   **500 g** **(16 oz)**

1 **large** basket of strawberries

EQUIPMENT:

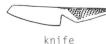
knife

LARGE
bowl

saucepan
(method 2)

large bowl
& whisk **(method 4)**

---

method 1

a glass of rosé *or* light red wine

+ 1 Tbsp of **SUGAR**

or

method 2

1 lemon *or* lime **+** 2 Tbsp of **SUGAR** **+** a sprig of fresh basil*

*rinsed

or method 3

of balsamic vinegar 1 Tbsp **+** 1 Tbsp of **SUGAR** **+** vanilla **ICE CREAM**

or

method 4

6 fl oz/¾ cup of heavy cream **+** 1 Tbsp of **SUGAR** **+** a glass of guava or mango *nectar*

RINSE &  HULL the strawberries. CUT into: 2   4 OR 6  *pieces, depending on their size.*

---

method 1:

PUT them into a **LARGE** bowl.

ADD:

the wine & *the sugar*

MIX *very gently* & *ideally,* LET STAND for 30 mins.

or method 2:

PUT: *the basil leaves* *the sugar* *a glass of water* into a small saucepan

BRING to a boil, stirring. SIMMER for 5 mins.

REMOVE the basil leaves, *a little* & ADD the lemon or lime juice.

Let it cool & *pour over the strawberries.*

or method 3:

STIR together the vinegar and sugar.

ADD to the strawberries & MIX gently.

LEAVE to MARINATE for about **30 mins.**

Serve with *vanilla* ice cream

or method 4:

POUR the cream into a large bowl and WHISK until it forms soft peaks. *whisk*

ADD 1 *tbsp* of **SUGAR.**

POUR the *fruit nectar* over the strawberries, ADD a little sugar and...

SERVE with the cream.

 nice 'n' fruity

34

Keda Black, the author:

Thank you to my two editors, Catie from London and Rosemarie à Paris.
And thank you Alice: beautiful work!

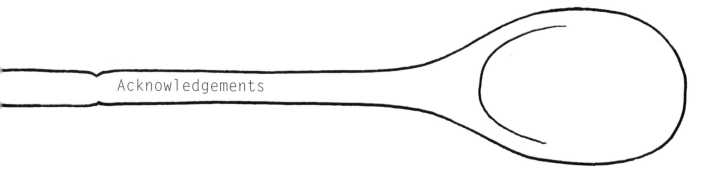

Acknowledgements

Alice Chadwick, the illustrator:

Thank you to S, G & P. x

Author: Keda Black
Photography: Deidre Rooney
Illustration: Alice Chadwick

First published by Marabout (Hachette Livre) in French in 2010
This edition published in 2011 by Lyons Press

Lyons Press is an imprint of Globe Pequot Press.

Library of Congress Cataloguing-in-Publication Data is available on file.

ISBN 978-0-7627-7896-6

Printed in China.

10 9 8 7 6 5 4 3 2 1

+ Survival Kit +

Of course, you can

survive

with a small camping stove and a kettle... Or with a microwave and a few plastic containers. But if you like to cook a little and hope not to eat the same thing all the time, then check out this list of (almost) essential pieces of kitchen gear.

To cook on the store:

about 4 quarts

a SAUCEPAN (small)

A LARGE SAUCEPAN OR STOCKPOT, with a lid!

&

A COLANDER

a frying pan

A MEDIUM SIZED FRYING PAN (8 in) preferably heavy and non-stick. Better to invest in a good quality one as the *cheap* ones wear out very quickly.

Cooking essentials:

micro **wave** *To microwave food:*

lid

MICROWAVABLE PLASTIC CONTAINERS of different sizes. They can double as lunchboxes (if the lids close tightly) or to keep leftovers in the fridge.

oven *To cook in a traditional oven:*

the oven GRILL

&

a rectangular or oval OVEN DISH